ONE BODY OF CHRIST

USING TECHNOLOGY TO BUILD THE ONE BODY OF CHRIST

STEVE@SMCCUTCHAN.COM

Primix Publishing
11620 Wilshire Blvd
Suite 900, West Wilshire Center, Los Angeles, CA, 90025
www.primixpublishing.com
Phone: 1-800-538-5788

Published by Primix Publishing: 02/12/2024

ISBN: 979-8-89194-062-8(sc)
ISBN: 979-8-89194-063-5(e)

Library of Congress Control Number: 2024901307

PRIMIX
PUBLISHING
THE WRITE CHOICE

ONE BODY OF CHRIST
A SPIRITUAL CONVERSATION

The Big Picture

DO YOU LIVE IN AN ANXIOUS SOCIETY?

Anxiety is a response to what William Butler Yeats spoke of in his poem *The Second Coming*: "Things fall apart, the center does not hold." When we feel the ground shift beneath our feet, whether personally or globally, it is as if we have lost control. Our sense of security dims, and we begin to feel helpless to affect the outcome.

Think about our society and the institutions which we have depended on to provide a sense of order and rationality to life. Whether through greed, arrogance, lust, or ignorance, what institution can you name that has not failed our trust in significant ways. If I say, "You can take that to the bank." does that build confidence in an era of failed financial institutions and recent stories of corporate greed. I recently saw a poll suggesting that only 13% are willing to say they "trust the government." It is not hard to find many people that believe the military lied with respect to some of the wars we have fought in recent years. The list can go on to include charities, educational institutions, businesses, and sadly, the church. It is as if things are falling apart and it is not clear that anyone has the power to change that.

Whether it is Moses as he faced the Red Sea, the Disciples following the crucifixion, or the church in our time, we are called to proclaim boldly a message of hope in a sea of uncertainty. There are no easy answers, and, as spiritual leaders, we are charged with bringing spiritual insight and the courage of faith for our members as they live their lives in our complex and evolving society and world.

This booklet offers you a unique way to take advantage of technology to build community both among your church members and with other churches around the world. The intention is to deepen members spiritual maturity and renew their vision of what it can mean to be part of the One Body of Christ provided with all necessary spiritual gifts to contribute to the healing of this fractured world.

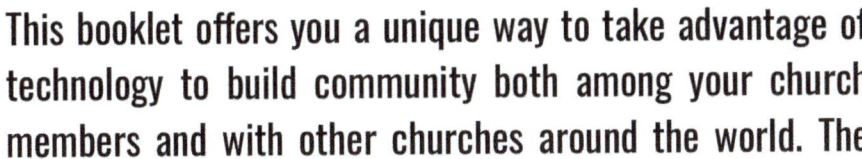

HIDING FROM VULNERABILITY

When our institutions fail us, people feel very vulnerable and anxious. You are asked to be a pastor to anxious people who feel like the world is out of control. From sports teams, to bankers, to government, to military, to educational institutions, to merchants, and the list can go on, who do you really trust? As a pastor, you can add the church who many people feel has also let them down.

So you come to a church with people whose experience has made them feel vulnerable and who don't trust anyone they can't see up close. Brene Brown, in her study on anxiety and vulernability suggests that people in such a situation try to numb the fears that make them feel bad. Some try to do it through drugs or sex, others by wealth or power, and still others by building a shield around them so they don't have to feel. The problem is that you can't selectively numb feelings, so you begin to shut down from all that gives life meaning and joy.

CONGREGATIONS OF SCARED PEOPLE

Brene Brown suggests 3 basic responses to vulnerability that we can easily see reflected in our churches. People want their church to offer clear and certain answers that help them feel secure. They want perfect institutions and people, so they have little tolerance for imperfection. They pretend that what they want is not secured at the cost to others. They want the church programs and pastor to attend to their needs, and they don't like being asked to think beyond themselves to the implications for the larger world. They may not say it, but they are scared, and they want to be reassured that someone has the perfect answer that will build the perfect community, and if others don't get it, that is their problem.

A SPIRITUAL CONVERSATION

What if you can use modern technology to connect your membership and engage them in a spiritual conversation that deepens their faith and offers them a vision of being called to be part of the One Body of Christ that reaches across the world. If we trust that God is the sovereign Lord of all creation and God has called the church to be a light unto the world, then members have a firmer foundation upon which to stand as they adjust to this rapidly changing world.

This book is designed to enable a single pastor to take the first step in proposing to his governing board that they initiate a process that encourages their members to reach out to each other through the internet. Then they will reach out to other churches and converse about their faith. These other churches can be anywhere in the country. They also can be anywhere in the world. The church can transcend miles of separation and celebrate together as the One Body of Christ.

FIRST STEPS

1. Read through this booklet and decide if this plan holds promise for you.
2. Explain the idea to your governing board and get their confirmation.
3. Identify 3 or 4 pastors in other states (or even another country) with which you will share the plan and invite them to agree to engage in the same process with their congregation. At least in this first experience, it will be best if the churches were of relatively same size.

I'm suggesting your first experience be with clergy in other states and another country because it will likely spark the interest and imagination of your membership.

Later, you can do it with other churches in your judicatory or churches of different denominations in your neighborhood. Each has their benefits.

If your governing board agrees, then together you make the following preparaton:

1. Identify two sets of members with special gifts; one with a gift in computer technology or information technology and a couple with a willingness to summarize the information you receive from your membership into a composite report.
2. Set up a separate email account for this project—like a Gmail account.

Second Step

Set up an invitation letter to your membership. Share it with your partner pastors so that you are sending the same invitation in all of your congregations.

You may adapt the following sample letter to explain the idea to your membership.

Sample letter

Dear _____

I have asked the Session (or your church governing board) to invite you to participate in what I hope will be an enlightening but also fun spiritual conversation among our membership. Since we live in an age of technology and instant communication, I propose that we try this through the internet. This also will enable us to also reach across the miles and share the composite response with congregations in other areas and cultures. It will be an enjoyable way to see our similarities and differences.

I want to engage our whole congregation in a spiritual conversation. The process is that over the next several months, I will send you a series of emails (one every couple of weeks and no more than six in total.) asking you to respond to some questions about your experience of the church and your own spiritual experience. In respecting the hectic pace of all our lives, I am asking you to hit respond button and reply with no more than two or three sentences to each question. This is intended to be a collection of your first visceral response. There will be time for deeper reflection later.

I have asked ??????????????????? to receive your responses sent to ????@gmail.com and to gather them into a composite response without names attached to create an image of our church body. The result will demonstrate both our diversity and commonality of faith.

Now here is a fun addition to our experience. I have contacted three other clergy who pastor in (name the states and one pastor in another country) to conduct the same survey of the membership of their congregations. Have you ever wondered if people in different sections of the country think differently than you do? What about in a different culture or country?

You are free not to make a response to any individual question posed, but I hope you will participate. It will be important to get as many members as possible to participate so that we can build a whole picture. Therefore, regardless of the level of your participation in our congregation, your response will help construct a complete picture.

I'm counting on all of us to be blessed by this experience.

Pastor's name

Third Step

When you have the project set up in your congregation and in the churches of your partner clergy, agree upon a calendar of when you will

1. Send the invitation letter to your membership.
2. Dates for sending each of the sets of questions to your respective membership.
3. Your plan for compiling and sharing your responses with each of your congregations.
4. The way that you will share the composite pictures with each other and your congregations.

Fourth Step

If the process is working and people are enjoying the process in both your and your partner congregations, there is an additional step that can increase both the fun and celebration of the oneness of the Body of Christ spread across the globe. Consult with your computer assistant in your congregations and explore the possibility of setting up a video-conference among your participating congregations. This shouldn't be expensive and it will allow your membership to identify with the other congregations even as they become more aware of the reflections of their own members.

The live conference can involve several elements.

1. There might be some limited testimony about how this experience has affected each of the congregations.
2. Each congregation might want to share the gift of music with the others—children's choir, adult choir, instrumentalists, vocal solos, etc..
3. Each congregation might identify ahead of time a particular need or ministry that the other congregations can include in prayer.
4. A litany based on an adaption of a psalm could be shared in affirming their mutual ministry and their common faith. (See Psalm 57 adapted below.)
5. This would be an excellent opportunity to celebrate communion together.
6. There might be some spontaneous expression of hopes for future experiences.

Prayer for our churches

PSALM 57 ADAPTED

Be merciful to our congregations, O God,

be merciful to each of our churches,

for in you our member's soul takes refuge;

In the shadow of your wings we all will take refuge,

until the destroying storms pass by.

Each of our churches cries to God Most high;

to God who fulfills his purpose for each of them.

God will send from heaven and save our members,

he will put to shame those who trample on their faith.

God will send forth his steadfast love and his faithfulness.

Our churches lie down among lions

that greedily devour human prey;

their teeth are spears and arrows,

their tongues sharp swords.

Be exalted, O God, above the heavens.

let your glory be over all the earth.

They set a net for our ministries steps;

Our church's soul was bowed down,

They dug a pit in a congregation's path,

but they have fallen into it themselves.

Our heart is steadfast, O God,

Our heart is steadfast

.

Our choirs will sing and make melody.

Awake, their soul! Awake, O harp and lyre!

Our music will awake the dawn.

Our members will give thanks to you, O Lord, among the peoples;

Together we will sing praises to you among the nations.

For your steadfast love is as high as the heavens;

your faithfulness extends to the clouds.

Be exalted, O God, above the heavens.

let your glory be over all the earth.

You can adapt other psalms to lift your prayers to God. Consider adapting Psalm 23 to address your joint celebration. More on the use of Psalms can be found in *Experiencing the Psalms* www.smccutchan.com

EXPLORING THE TYPES OF QUESTIONS TO BE USED IN THE SURVEYS

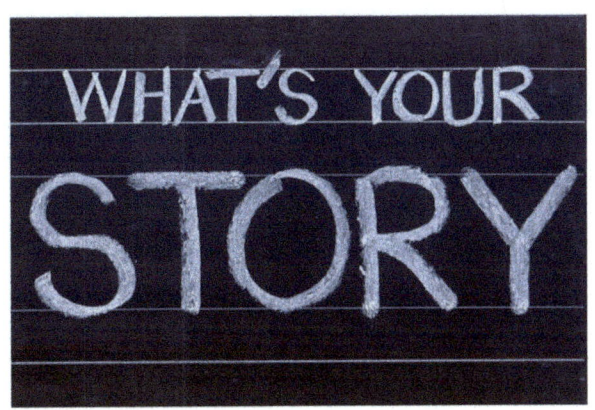

I would encourage you to begin with some questions that would be relatively easy to answer in short, succinct responses. As you begin, you will want answers that can be brought together to form a picture of the congregation. You also want to begin with questions that don't make the responders uncomfortable.

It is important that you and your partner clergy agree from the beginning which questions you will use. Later in the process, you can discuss adding new questions, but here are some samples for the initial survey of your respective congregations.

You might also want to include the suggestion that they imagine how their church's composite response might differ with that of the other participating congregations.

CONSIDER THE FOLLOWING POSSIBILITIES.

- What are two things you would be most pleased to have other churches know about your church?
- If you could change ONE SMALL THING about your church, what would it be?
- What two subjects about faith would you like to see sermons address in your congregation?
- Of all the things Jesus taught, what are two of the most important ones for our church to reflect in our life together?
- If God has a particular call for your church, how would you describe it? Are you having an opportunity to be faithful to that calling? What might help you in that regard?
- If all Christian churches proclaim and emphasize one of Jesus' teachings, what would you choose? To what degree do you think you can support emphasizing that belief in your own church?
- If Jesus prayed that his disciples should love one another like he had loved them, John 13:34-35 , how should churches behave towards other churches to witness to that belief? What is the message that such behavior would convey to the rest of society?
- **Spiritual Gifts:** Paul mentions 9 spiritual gifts in Galatians 5:22-23.
  - Love,
  - joy,
  - peace,
  - patience,
  - kindness,
  - generosity,
  - faithfulness,
  - gentleness, and
  - self control.

Which two or three of these gifts do you see most exhibited
by some members of this church
and by the church as a whole?

As you will note, the churches grow progressively deeper as they proceed. They also progress to reflecting on your church as part of the larger Body of Christ. This is where your connection with the other churches becomes even more important.

Imagine as a pastor how you might benefit from hearing how your members respond to such questions.

I would suggest that you use percentages when reporting the results of your conversation. For example, you might report that 40% wanted the church to increase their knowledge of Scripture, 20% wanted to become involved in ministries of compassion, and 30 % wanted to become more involved in ministries of compassion, etc. This both allows members to recognize the diversity of the congregation and avoids thinking of the responses as a contest of votes.

Share your summary of results with the whole congregation. Also, tell them that they will soon hear about similar results from the other congregations.

ANSWERING JESUS' COMMAND

"I give you a new commandment, that you love one another... By this, everyone will know that you are my disciples if you have love for one another." John 13:34-35 This booklet is designed to guide you in one step that you can take to obey Jesus command that the disciples of Christ love one another and demonstrate to the world how we build community in a fractured world.

By making use of the connectivity of the internet, we can reach out to all of the expressions of the Body of Christ around the world and build a community of hope. We do not need to be restrained by distance, denominational identity, or cultural differences. And, you don't have to wait for someone else to do it. It doesn't require large numbers, large organizations, power, wealth, or fame. An individual can be led by God's Spirit from any place in the world and make a positive difference.

If you want to be that person, and I can help you, please feel free to contact me at stephenmccutchan@gmail.com .